STRANGERS

ANTHOLOGY OF POETRY

Maria Cowen

Table Of Contents

Introduction

Poems in the Strangers Anthology of Poetry are more than a simple overflow of mystical experience; they are an artistic creation of the highest craftsmanship as well. Nonetheless, the divine tone that pervades Maria's work undeniably owes its presence also to the mystical experience.

Maria didn't learn about poetry but practiced composing her own poems. It all happened one night, when some window in the universal fabric opened and the poems started pouring down, one after another, keeping her awake all night. By morning she was exhausted but had a big stack of notes taken during this outbreak of creativity.

Out of the heavenly character of Maria's poetry, flows love and hope, and we can't help noting that the inspiration didn't seem to be of this world.

Always turning within as a tool for expressing her own experience, Maria does not surprise us by the way her exalted poetry resonates with the Universal Love. This inspired feeling is always a primary source for her.

Discovering in poetry a means for celebrating mystical insights and other special occasions, she introduced to her readers the profound concepts in the form of verses. In addition, like a greeting card, poems represent for her a simple way of sending a special message to her readers.

She came to realize that these symbolic expressions of poetry could also provide an excellent introduction into the intimate knowledge of the mystery of the Soul. In some of her poems, Maria contemplates the great secrets of the Divine; in the rest, she speaks of her own spiritual experiences, which also bear an inspiring content.

The poems sing of the happiness that comes from life in harmony with the Soul, detachment, and a love that grows in deep knowledge and connection with the infinite.

Heart Of An Emerald

Cool is the heart of the emerald
Cool like depths of the ocean
When I walk its green avenues
I can feel its heartbeat
Then the awareness stirs slowly
And the emerald wakes from its emerald dreams,
And talks to me about its mysteries
About his birth
Millions of years ago
Beneath the mother mountain,
Then washed by the mountain stream
Into the hands of the explorer,
Polished on the wheel he suffered
But acquired a clearer vision
Through the brilliant facets;
Witnessed rise and fall of the empires.
Passed through thousands of hands
Admired by countless people
Who lived and died
To make room for new generations
And he was already losing hope
That someone will discover
That he was alive

Until he rested upon my palm
And taught me his secrets;
Since that day
I look for heart
In all things
In the trees and stones, and lakes
And since that day
I'm never alone again.

The Justice

If I could steal the gold
From the sunset
And pour it into my cup
I would be
Gold and beautiful
And full of glory.
But what would become
Of the sunset
Robbed of its splendour
It would change into the night
And boundless darkness
Where my stolen beauty
Would be seen no more
And all my effort
Would be in vain;
So whenever you take
Something that belongs to another,
Don't expect to profit from it
Because it will turn bitter in your mouth,
And unless you give it back
Where it belongs
You will know no peace, nor enjoyment.

Love Search

Last night, I saw in my dream
Your face full of sorrow,
Your eyes were full of tears
Because you couldn't find me;
But my dear love
This is only because
All this time
You are looking in the wrong places
I am here
I have always been here
For you to come and find me
So wipe your tears
And look inside your heart for guidance;
Your heart will lead you
To your only true love,
Your twin flame
That never dies
You and I
Made of the same substance,
Parts of the same great flame
Which is our mother and father
The source of all beings;
Look into your heart my love
I'm there to help you
Find your way.

Change

I am a single grain of sand
In the endless desert
An insignificant grain
Like millions of others forming the desert
I have been here for thousands of years
Burnt by the merciless sun,
Swept by the winds
Enduring all
And one day
A pilgrim's foot crushed me
And a single tear of despair
Fell upon me
And a miracle happened
For I grew and blossomed
I realized I was a seed
That could change the face of the desert
But the sun and the wind were stronger
Then a single sprout of hope;
I died.... but..... I didn't die completely
I returned to be a grain of sand
In the endless desert.
But now I know
That even if I have to wait

Another thousand upon thousand years
There will be another pilgrim
To come my Way
And shed a life-giving tear
I will wait
And the next time
I'll try harder
I will know better
How to survive
And then I shall change a face of my world.

Well Of Knowledge

I dip my mind
Into the well of knowledge
And drink deeply, hungrily.
But unless my mind is ready
To understand and absorb
The mysteries of all times,
I shall remain thirsty
Until the next time
I have a chance to drink again.

Eye Of A Hurricane

I am in an eye of a hurricane
The only calm place there is
In the midst of destruction
All around me.
I witness
Everything being swept and crushed
To pieces
But cries of pain don't reach me
And pleading for help doesn't matter
For I'm unmoved and still
Because I'm in an eye of a hurricane.

Magic Mirror

Calm are the waters of my mind today
Therefore, I can see on the surface
A reflection of moon and of a thousand stars
And also answers to all my questions.
But when the water is stirred
And the calmness disturbed
You only see the broken image
And get but false answers
And you despair
Because nothing is right any more
But then all you have to do
Is calm the waters
It is so simple.

MARIA COWEN

The Rain

Let the silver drops of rain
Fall upon your head
To penetrate deep
Into the hidden parts of your soul
Where the dark thoughts dwell
And let them be washed away
All those small and unworthy things
You stored there for so long
And only when your soul is clean
You will feel free
To receive a real gift
Of the silver rain
To fill the golden cup
With crystalline water
So you don't have to long
For another rain.

MARIA COWEN

Rebirth

In the darkness
All things are born
To come to this world
With a cry of pain,
Then strive laboriously
To get bigger and better
Only to return to the darkness
At the end of their days.
But don't you fear the darkness
Because it's an end
But it's also a beginning
Of all things
Waiting to be born again
To be better
Every time they come back.

The Wave

A big wave came
And swept me away
From the safety of the shore
Into the endless abyss.
Shall I blame the wave
For my misfortune
Or my own ignorance
For letting the wave catch me,
For playing to close with the danger
And shall I keep looking
For someone to blame
And drown in my indecision
Instead of catching the next wave
Rolling toward the safety of the shore?

Love

Love is a song
My heart sings
When it's in harmony
With the Universe.
When the harmony is lost
Love is also lost
Replaced by discord and frustration.
So don't let the harmony be disturbed,
Guard it as the most precious thing
You will ever have;
And once you elevate yourself
In a perfect love
Let the others
Bathe in the pool of your happiness
Let them drink from your precious vessel
And share with them your love freely
And your vessel will always be full
For such is a miracle of love.

Strangers

I don't know you
And yet, I have known you since the beginning of time.
So close your eyes
And come to the dark place
Halfway between the dream and reality
And there I am, waiting,
A spark of life
As small as a grain of sand
In the endless desert....
But I also am all things,
A universe that knows no limit.
That's why I know you
Because you have been a part of me all along...
Without knowing.

God's Will

I have my hands full
Of golden grains of wheat
Shall I bake bread
And feed the hungry
Or shall I sow the seed
And grow more wheat?
And so are we
In the hands of God
Whichever way He decides
Our fate to be
Everything will serve the higher purpose
Nothing is ever wasted.

Listen

On the hot summer day
Alone in the fields
I put my ear to the ground
To listen for my father's footsteps
But then I start hearing other things.
I hear a drop of water falling to the ground
Fertilizing the seed
Sleeping in the dark earth
And I witness one of the mysteries of the Universe.
That's how most things are learned,
By accident.
So just keep listening
For whatever insignificant thing it might be
And you might just discover
The answer to all your questions.

The Seed

We are like seeds
Buried in the fertile soil
Waiting for our chance to blossom.
But unless we reach out for the sun
We will remain seeds forever.
Maybe I'll grow to be a single blade of grass,
Or maybe I'll grow to be a tree
To give shade to the sea of grass.
There is no way
For the grass to outgrow the tree
But all things have their own purpose....
For who would the tree give his shade to
If there wasn't any grass....

Two In One

Woman and man in one
Are the ultimate perfection.
Being just one
We are incomplete
Like being just half
Of the great whole;
So we must search
For the other half
That would fit.
We might discard many halves
That don't fit
Quite as good
Until we find
The right one
And become whole again.

Promised Land

They promised us
A land of milk and honey.
We waited for millennia
Despairing and swearing
That we were cheated
Out of the golden age,
Our rightfull heritage lost.
But than,
Didn't they tell us
That it's not enough
To lean back and wait,
Letting everything go wrong
Around us?
Didn't they tell us
That we were to be the makers
Of the golden age
If we only tried?

Thoughts

All thoughts
Born in your minds
Have a life of their own
Have a substance
And are like our babies
They live in the plane
Parallel to ours
Where all things are formed
Before they manifest
In flesh
In our material plane;
Some of your thoughts
Are like jewel butterflies
Full of glory.
But some born of fear and doubt
Are like bats
That fly out to feed
Upon other people's thoughts
Beware of this predator
Be careful what you think

Butterfly

A rainbow butterfly flew
And sat on my heart
Seeking warmth of my love
And my heart swelled in admiration
Of her beauty and brilliance
And radiated the love
The butterfly was craving for
And nurtured and happy
She flew away.
But then a cockroach
Run under my feet
And I crushed it
Under my heel
With disgust.
But then a wave of shame and pity
Swept over my being
For what is the difference
Between the cockroach and the butterfly....
They both want to live
As I do.

The Star

I am a little dim star
At the end of the universe
I look at the big radiant stars
And envy them their brightness
And I blame them
That they have stolen the light
That belongs to me....
I cry and suffer
But they shine with their brilliant indifference
Ignoring me....
And I feel hurt, betrayed and cheated;
But since nobody seems to care
I'm forced to look into myself
And there I discover the reason
Of my miseries
For instead of wasting my energies
On hate and envy
I should have used my strength
To nurture my own self.
Aren't we all like stars
On the night sky
Some brighter, some dimmer
Depends how deep we can drink
From the source
Which has roots in our hearts.

Light And Darkness

It is so good
To see the light again
When you come back
From the darkness.
But one wouldn't exist
Without another
And one day
When your eyes will grow weary
From looking at the light
You can return
To the darkness
And rest.

Hiding

Didn't anyone tell you
That hiding your head
In the pile of sand
Won't solve your problem,
No matter
How deep you bury it
And how tight
You keep your eyes shut?
So open your eyes
And gather your courage
And look your problem
Straight in the face,
Examine it
And then you will realize
That it wasn't as bad
As you thought it was
And that the solution can be found
So all will be well
At the end.

Islands

A handful of sparkling jewels
Cast upon the face of the timeless ocean
By the hand of God
They dream their endless dreams
Clouds caressing their mountain peaks,
Waves lulling them to sleep....
And they are unaware
Of thousands of tiny human insects
Crawling on their surface.....
Until the human insects
Start drilling the islands
To the very core of their being
Looking for treasures
And who knows what else
Ready to rip the reaches
Out of the islands heart
And then the islands will wake
From their slumber, angry,
Shake the intruders off
And spit the fire upon them.
If you walk the islands
Preserve and respect their beauty.
Don't cut the branch you sit on.

Walking In Spirit

When I walk in spirit
Every night
I visit places
I know from other lifetimes
I talk to people
That are close to my soul
And I receive a guidance
From my God Self
Watching over my Lower Self
With love and pity
To pick me up
Every time I stumble.
My spirit flies high
Free of bonds....
I can go to explore
Furthest corners of the universe....
As long as I return
To my shell at dawn....
But some spirits
Are like blind birds
That fly beating their heads
Against the cliffs
In dark despair and hopelessness....

If you encounter such spirit
In your nightly wanderings
Show him the way
To the light

The Vision

I am standing
On top of the snowy mountain peak
Looking down
And it is almost painful
To see so much beauty below....
And a single tear of happiness
Falls upon the snow
And melts it
And a drop of water
Full of rainbows
Slides down the slopes,
Down to the lush valley
Rolls upon the plain
To meet a cool, clear spring.
A weary pilgrim
Dipped his parched lips.
In the spring to drink
And tasted the salt of my tear
And looked up amazed
And our eyes met
He thought he had a vision
But what he really saw
Was his future

After a long struggle
To climb the mountain
To face a thorny way up
To reach the heights
Of enlightenment

Limitations

When you say
I can't do it!
It's impossible!
I'm not able to!
It can never be!
You are imprisoning your spirit
Wrapping it in the net of impossibilities
Putting a blindfold
Around your eyes
Paralyzing all action,
Becoming a slave
To your ignorance,
Conditioning yourself
To helplessness and failure.
If you only knew
That there are no limits
Neither, in time, nor space
Of what you can do
As a spirit
If you only learn
To leave your body
And soar high
Free!!!

Visitation

I shall come to you one night
Invisible
Hover over your bed
While you sleep
Brush your forehead
With a gentle kiss
And you might think
It is a breeze
And I'll sit on your pillow
And whisper into your ear
And you will think
You are dreaming
Or imagining things
And when you hear the old closet croaking
And the clock will ring midnight
And there will be footsteps
Around your bed
In the darkness
And the shiver will run down your spine
Will you be afraid
Or will you know
That this is just me?

Moon Song

In the dark, I stir
And open my eyes
I stretch and purr
And my whiskers twitch
With a strange anticipation
And excitement.
This is an hour of the spirits
I feel them all around me
In the darkness
Flying about their business
As usual
As I go about mine.
I jump through the Window
And there my love
Waits for me
And we sit together
And sing our joy
To the full moon
For this is our way
To express our love
For life and all living things
And our participation
In the infinite
But then someone throws the stone
And breaks the spell.

Seeing Yourself

They rub their eyes
And open them wide to see,
And yet see nothing.
But those who close their eyes
And look inward
Discover the riches
Beyond their wildest dreams.
Those are the ones that can really see.
For only in your heart
You can see
How you really are,
With no deception and no lie.
Your hart will tell you
What the truth is
If you just learn to listen.
So smash you mirror
And stop looking for your image
Through your friends' eyes.
You don't need to fool yourself
Any longer
Because what you'll find
In your inward search
Will be much better

Than any false image
You created for yourself
Before.
So if they say
"You can't see in the dark"
Don't believe them.
For it is only in the dark
That you can really see.
So close your eyes.

Word To Word

From a grain of sand to a desert
Of a thousand dunes
Breathing out the noon heat,
From a drop of water to an ocean
Undulating
In its blue majesty,
From a man to the Universe
Dazzling
With richness of its forms,
From an atom to a galaxy
Spinning slowly
In a twinkling of countless stars,
From the heat of a loving heart
To the great and unbeatable force
Fusing the Universe,
And binding all that exists together,
From one human soul to the Creator
Passing His breath
Through all living creatures.
Such inseparable dependencies,
Inextricable in the process of existence
Which is called Life.
Because the desert would not be so

If not for the grains of sand,
And the ocean would not be
If not for the drops of water,
The Universe would not be the Universe
If it was lacking man,
Galaxies would not exist without atoms
And the Universe would cease
If lacking that
Binding force
Called Love.
But those human souls –
- They are the shards of the Creator,
And if not He,
Who by His Will's fancy,
From one word to another,
Made the particles of the Universe move
Until from darkness and emptiness
Life hatched...
If not He,
The Protector of Higher Order,
Only General Chaos
Would be...

Thorns and Roses

Why does a man
Who thinks himself the king of Creation
Inflict pain on others?
Why does he hurt and persecute,
Thrust thorns into innocent hearts?
Is it because of stupidity, not knowing
That he hurts others?
Or is it on purpose
Out of cruelty, hate and envy?
Does he make people suffer
Because it gives him pleasure?
But regardless if it's a thorn
Of a stupid one or the cruel,
Piercing the heart
Kills just the same.
So wouldn't the world be a better place
If instead of thorns
Roses hug close to the hearts,
Relieve and silence
Pain and sorrow on earth
And the subtle aroma of roses
Would permeate everything
Bringing beauty

And love of brother to brother
Thorns and roses from the same branch grow
On the tree of feelings and emotions
The choice is always ours
Fools will choose thorns
But those who love the world and its people
Surely will always choose roses....

Native Pride

I'm proud to be born of this land,
To be a native son of America
I'm proud of my roots
That reach far into the past
As far as the land itself can remember
And I'm proud of my people's wisdom
Which we shall keep alive
For as long as we last
From my pride, I draw a great strength to survive
The so-called progress
To protect my native land
From the greedy and the disrespectful
Today a call to all my brothers
To celebrate life
With all the creatures of our land
With deer and owl and the wolf
As we did in the old times
Let's merge with the Great Spirit
Unite in his wisdom
And sing the glory and pride
For we are his children
And this is our native land.

Light and Shadows

Where – after a short winter's day
Dusk falls quickly
And embraces ground
Ossified by darkness;
Where people
Wander
Shrouded in darkness
Like shadows
At the Elysian Fields...
There, in a dark, cold
Corner
Two souls squatted
With sorrow in their
Hearts
And a longing for light;
United in their
Misery
They clung to
Each other
Searching for support,
Searching for comfort,
Searching for the tiniest bit
Of warmth.
And both would like to ascend
But are scared of the dark –
Darkness entwines them

Fear paralyses them
Angst hinders their
Wings.
And so they would have
Long remained,
These two souls
In ossified fear
If one of them hadn't suddenly
Noticed
A little, shy light
Flickering in freezing puffs
Of Northern Wind
Somewhere
Deep
In the depths
Of its companion in misery
Soul.
Look!
Look!
The soul flickered
In joyful excitement
Look, light
From the very core
Of your existence
Look!!!
Oh, indeed
The other soul was
Aghast,
And as it looked
Into this tiny glow
The light shone
Stronger and brighter,
Lighting up the darkness
Suffocated by fright

With
Its brightness.
The other soul
Moved closer
To warm
In the light,
In the brightness reflecting
From its companion.
Suddenly it noticed
A flickering
In itself…
And when both souls'
Sparkling shine grew bigger,
And were lit proudly
By their inner light,
One whispered to the other:
"Come, we must
Tell the others about it"

Language Of Nature

Who said
That trees do not speak?
That their leaves
Do not whisper to one another
Sharing the latest
Tree gossip...
And that fragrant needles of spruce
Do not ring
When they laugh
Together with the wind?
Who said
That the pine will not sob
Under a woodcutter's axe
And suffer
'Till the very last drop
Of scented resinous blood
Is drawn?
Who said
That a stone will not sigh,
Longing for the sun
While waiting for the morning
With hope
That it will be embraced,

Warmed,
by its life-giving rays?
Who said
The earth will not groan
When raped
With a thrust into her inside
So to steal her treasures?
Who said
That the sun does not surround us
With its love,
Bathing us tenderly
In its golden light,
Giving us warmth and life?
Who said
That stars
Twinkling at us
Do not reveal
Their deepest secrets
Of distant,
Unreachable
Cosmic space?
Who said
That silence
Is not a harmony of sound
Swirling with beauty,
And where it swirls
With a fullness of life
We see only emptiness?
Who said
That every man's soul

Does not sing
Its very own
Unrepeatable song
Which weaves into
A choir of other souls
In the process of the creation
Of the Universe?
Or maybe
We haven't yet learned to
Look…. hear….. And feel….?

MARIA COWEN

Journey Into The Depth Of Soul

The deeper I penetrate into the depth of my soul
The more I find in me
Goodness and beauty,
The bigger treasures I discover,
Glittering like precious gems,
In the murky depth of my existence
And I see clearly
That only on the surface
Like a thin frozen shell
Surrounding my being
Is a layer of fears and insecurities,
Prejudice and anger
Resentments and grievances
And deeper under this shell
Lives my subconscious
In the form of dark space
Where from time to time
A spark of light flashes
Shooting towards some unknown
Destination and goal
And when I completely submerge
And lose myself
In those murky spaces

Inevitably
As if thou under the influence
Of some unknown force of attraction
At last I arrive to a place
Where my soul slumbers...
And when I concentrate on it
All my attention
It will awake
And shine brighter and brighter
With the warm glow
Gentle
But also strong and penetrating.
And this light/glow
All the far corners
And suddenly
All will become clear
There'll be no more questions
Nor doubts
And only one feeling
Will fill me to the brink
And only one thought
Will dominate my consciousness
Love without boundaries
Nor limitations
Omnipresent
Resplendent
Uniting everything
That lives and breathes
Into one great family
Called the Brotherhood of Illuminated Souls

Blind Birds

Where does it hide from me
The sense of life,
Its meaning and purpose?
What is most important
In a man's life...?
Where can I find
Answers
To my questions...?
Beneath a roadside stone...,
Reflected in water...,
In your eyes...?
Or maybe somewhere
Far away
Beyond the distant horizon...?
Sometimes
The understanding feels near
But when I try to catch it,
It escapes
Every time
Intangible like wind....
And still I search,
Wander through space,
Lands and seas so wide

Meeting others
On my way.
They search, too,
And like me, cannot find.
And like blind birds
With flight uncertain
From place to place
We wander,
Hurting our wings
On the sharp edges of failures
And bitter disappointments
We come across
In this desperate
Search.
And so I would have surely
My whole life spent
Searching for
Elusive truths
Like a blind bird
That doesn't know
What it's searching for
And where it'll get in time,
If one day
I hadn't met
A wise man,
Far away on a distant land,
And fell at his feet
Tired of wandering
Asking for a good word.
The wise man looked

Mercifully upon me,
Shook his grey head
And said:
"What you are looking for,
Pilgrim,
You could have found
Years ago
Without setting foot
Outside your homeland,
If only you had known that
That which you look for
You will find only
Within your own heart.
It goes by the name of... Love..."
The wise man touched my temple
Gently
And walked away...
And I, as waking
From a sleepy haze,
Understood immediately
The sense of my existence.

Architects Of Destiny

Are you the architect of your destiny,
A builder of your happiness,
A proud representative of the race of winners?
Or are you perhaps a victim of fate
A helpless toy in the hands of higher forces
Tossed into the corner of existence
When a capricious fate
Seemed to get tired of you
Or found another toy
To attract all its attention...?
But know that even if you are
A lost soul,
A victim of fate
Don't despair.
Believe me
You still can become the architect
And stand at the helm of your destiny
If only you can gather
Enough will power
And resilience
In the constant, never-ending
Work on yourself
To lift yourself

Once and for all
From your own weaknesses
And ignorance
And step-by-step going
Towards perfection.

Crumbs Of Happiness

Can you satisfy
The hunger of your soul
By picking at crumbs of happiness
Along the path of your life...?
Can you quench
The thirst of your heart
By drinking teardrops
Shed by others...?
Can your life
Be full
If you live
With hunger and thirst,
Unfulfilled,
Suffering...?
And, do you know
That the irony of your fortune
And all your pain
Comes only from
Your ignorance...?
For if you are able
Only for a moment to
Silence a sobbing heart
And complaining soul

Then having listened to your own self
Will you not hear sound
Somewhere deep in darkness
At the very bottom of your existence...?
Focus,
And listen carefully,
And you will recognize this strange hum
Alien, but at the same time
Oddly familiar.
Just there
In the deepest abyss
Of your being
Life-giving spring bursts out
A spring which tries to reach
The surface of your conscience
To satisfy the hunger
Of your soul
And to quench the thirst of your heart
The spring's deep roots
Reach into our
Longed for
Yet forgotten home
To the Ocean of Light
And now, since you know
How to satiate your soul
How to inebriate your heart
Bend no more
Pick not at scraps of happiness
Left by others,
For the well of true happiness

Swells in yourself
And when drinking of it
Do not forget about those
Who are thirsty
But don't offer them scraps
Rather, show them the way
To their own spring
Which waits in each of them
For the day of the great discovery…

Homeless Hearts

Homeless hearts
Like yellowed leaves
In the fall wind,
Shards thrown by fortune
From place to place
Homeless hearts
Rejected and hurt
Suffering in loneliness
Somewhere
In dark corners
Where the devil says goodnight,
Homeless hearts
Lost
Begging for an ounce of warmth
Hungry for love
Homeless hearts!
You will find shelter here
Here, there is always
A corner and comfort for you
Do you hear me calling??!!
Can I reach you
With my invitation???
Where? Where? The homeless

Hearts flattered
With waking
Shy hope
Where is our lost home?
Our family?
Our loved ones?
Here, here...
Here is the corner for the battered souls
Come and drink from the spring
Of bottomless love...

Like A Boat On The Restless Ocean

Have you ever seen
In dreams or when awake
The lonely sail of a boat
Lost amongst a turbulent ocean,
A fragile shell
Fighting against the raging waves
Threatening to crush it,
To sink it
In the unfathomable abyss?
Have you heard
A desperate flap of a sail
Lashed by wind,
Clatter of waves
Madly pounding at the deck,
Groan of joins
And creaks of wood
Under the pressing elements?
Have you then felt a fear
Of doom,
A desperate impulse of resignation,
Giving in to nature's power
Against which
The brittle boat

Has no chance of survival?
Or that may be what you,
An incidental observer,
Might think….
Have you then considered
How great the similarity
Between this lonely sail
And a man's fortune,
Who sails through the ocean of life
Coast to coast….
There are many seas and oceans
Governed by capricious moods….
On some
Many boats will sail
Their sails will meet
And pass
Sometimes
They will turn to the same port…
On other
Less travelled courses
One will sail alone.
Some of us
Sail through calm waters,
Others
Seem to fight
Along their way
Against the elements.
Some will sink,
Others
Drift hopelessly

With a broken mast,
Just to crush
Against the first rock they meet...
Now you will ask me
Upon what a boat's fortune depends?
On the ocean?
On the sailor?
Or maybe on the boat -
Its construction,
Its resistance?
The first requirement
Of survival is the boat itself,
Its robustness and its endurance.
That which is
Above the waters
Swept by winds
And lashed by waves
Is human consciousness
It is a real life,
Everyday life
With its thousands of everyday affairs,
Failures,
Small victories
And minor defeats...
In a nutshell
It is the part of a man
Which participates
In the so called
"Real life"...
The part of the beat

Beneath the water
Is human sub-consciousness
The world of daydreams
And delusions
A world of dreams
And hopes...
It is an aspect of a man
Somehow living
In a different dimension,
Submerged
In a different reality...
The mast and sail
Is human intuition
Stretched
And flapping
Between faith
And man's will,
The natural tendency
To survive,
To sail forward
To any
Distant destination.
The intuition
Which is a decisive power
And driving force...
These three components
Joined together
Harmoniously
Are able to withstand
The elements...

'Wait, wait...' you will say
'Let's not forget about the sailor!
Is he not the most important?
Is it not he who directs the boat?
Makes the right decisions?
Handles the sail and navigates
Like a virtuoso
Playing
An immortal symphony!!!?
'And who is the sailor?
You will ask impatiently
'My dear!
You are right
The sailor is here the most important.
Yet, if you haven't found out
For yourself
Listen carefully
To the voice of your heart,
For it is the heart that is a man's skipper
And his navigator
Leading the boat
Safely
Through the tumultuous
Ocean of life
Coast to coast...
It is best,
Safest,
To sail
With a heart filled with love...
Storms then are not dreadful,

The waves can be overcome,
And the bigger,
And greater the love is,
The greater obstacles the boat
Will conquer,
The more seas it will sail
And will safely visit many ports.
If you are
A good sailor,
Maybe one day
You will find
Your silent haven
Somewhere
On a distant
Restless ocean.

For The Reader

After all is said and done, what is the reward for the readers? After reading this anthology, was there comfort? Did the reader learn anything? Did they look deeper into their soul and reach some sort of better understanding of life, a purpose of existence? Did some fragments fall into place and achieve a greater harmony with the whole?

If so, I'm rewarded beyond my expectations.

I wish you all the best of luck on your path.

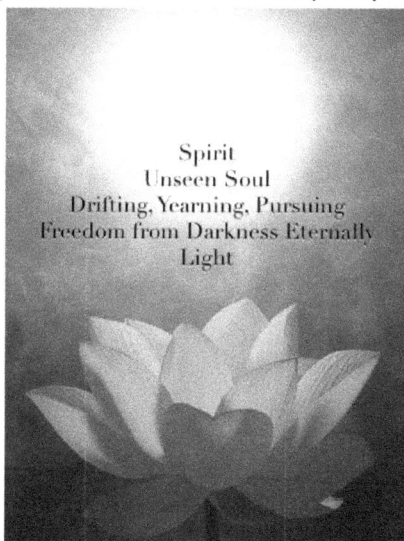

Spirit
Unseen Soul
Drifting, Yearning, Pursuing
Freedom from Darkness Eternally
Light

Learn to look for **inspiration** in unexpected places.

www.ingramcontent.com/pod-product-compliance
Lightning Source LLC
Chambersburg PA
CBHW071825020426
42331CB00007B/1608